Dear Mary

ALSO BY RUPERT M LOYDELL

Impossible Songs [with Sarah Cave] (Analogue Flashback 2017)
Love Songs for an Echo (Original Plus 2016)
Reasons (Hesterglock 2015)
The Return of the Man Who Has Everything (Shearsman Books 2015)
Esophagus Writ [with Daniel Y Harris] (Knives Forks and Spoons Press 2014)
Ballads of the Alone (Shearsman Books 2013)
Encouraging Signs. Interviews, essays and conversations (Shearsman Books 2013)
Tower of Babel (Like This Press, 2013)
Leading Edge Control Technology (Knives Forks & Spoons Press 2013)
Voiceover (Riverine) [with Paul Sutton] (Knives Forks and Spoons Press 2012)
Wildlife (Shearsman Books 2011)
A Music Box of Snakes [with Peter Gillies] (Knives Forks and Spoons Press 2010)
The Fantasy Kid (Salt Publications 2010)
Boombox (Shearsman Books 2009)
Lost in the Slipstream (Original Plus 2009)
An Experiment in Navigation (Shearsman Books 2008)
Ex Catalogue (Shadow Train 2006)
A Conference of Voices (Shearsman Books 2004)
The Museum of Light (Arc Publications 2003)

AS EDITOR:

Yesterday's Music Today [with Mike Ferguson] (Knives Forks and Spoons Press 2015)
Smartarse (Knives Forks and Spoons Press 2011)
From Hepworth's Garden Out (Shearsman Books 2010)
Troubles Swapped for Something Fresh: manifestos and unmanifestos
                    (Salt Publications 2009)

Rupert M Loydell

Dear Mary

Shearsman Books

First published in the United Kingdom in 2017 by
Shearsman Books
50 Westons Hill Drive
Emersons Green
BRISTOL
BS16 7DF

Shearsman Books Ltd Registered Office
30–31 St. James Place, Mangotsfield, Bristol BS16 9JB
(this address not for correspondence)

www.shearsman.com

ISBN 978-1-84861-519-9

*The drawing on page 12 is
'Esoteric Annunciation', copyright © A C Evans*

Contents

Preface

When you walk into the old schoolroom in Monterchi, where Piero della Francesca's *Madonna del Parto* is now displayed, the lights come on, sensing your motion. And for a moment, it is as if the two angels who hold open the little pavilion where the pregnant Mary stands have suddenly illuminated the whole world by uncovering the place where God has chosen to live.

Afterwards, as your eyes get used to the light, the painting, smaller than you expect and yet infinitely monumental (and how better to describe the Incarnation?) starts to give itself up.

First come its soft greens and deep reds, blues and traces of brocade, the silvery-grey fur lining of Mary's tent, all miraculously fresh, caught in the plaster of the cemetery chapel like the hazy colours of the hour either side of dawn. Then come its careful lines, its cleverness in framing, out of dead flatness, all the fleshy comfort of the world in three, crisp perspectival dimensions and more than three others of thought and word and deed.

It takes time to see. You walk towards it to find traces of Piero's hand in the brush strokes, in the drawing of each contour, the economy of the foreshortened feet, the singularity of each feather. You walk away again and sit on the bench to try to see the whole, to stop your eye darting between the parts, to imagine beyond the outer edges of the surviving fresco into the place where Piero made it.

Despite the physical loss to the painting, though, the most striking absence in the *Madonna del Parto* is that of Christ. The Virgin is not supposed to come without the child, and if she does it should not be alone but as visitor to her cousin Elizabeth. An iconography of Mary alone and pregnant, even as serenely self-possessed as this (perhaps because she is as serenely self-possessed as this) is disturbing. This is the Mary whom Joseph wondered about leaving, the Mary he feared would bring shame on him, the Mary whose baby had been made in his own absence.

When Donatello came to make that moment of making, in the Cavalcanti *Annunciation* at Santa Croce in Florence, he did so in the plainest of plain stone. The gritty sandstone he used, whose obduracy Dante had compared to that of his Florentine countrymen, only later came to acquire its poetic name *pietra serena*.[1] When Donatello carved it, it was still called

---

[1] Describing the Florentine descendants of the inhabitants of Fiesole, his friend Ser Brunetto Latini tells Dante of the proverbial, residual hardness they retained after descending from the hills; 'tiene ancor del monte e del macigno' – 'still keeping something of the mountain and the rock'. Dante Alighieri, *La Commedia secondo l'antica vulgata:* ed. Giorgio Petrocchi, 4 vols., (Milan, 1966-7), vol. II, *Inferno,* Canto XV, line 63, p. 249.

macigno, the stuff of millstones, of industry, the stuff of the city and its people, of a joke about worthless rocks in Boccaccio.[2]

Macigno makes the Cavalcanti *Annunciation* a vernacular and singularly Florentine object, more so than if it had been carved from marble. It speaks to the *fiorentinità* of its patrons and of its sculptor and consequently is an object of place, specifically and precisely, the incarnation in Florence and the Incarnation of Florence. Yet, having made his annunciation from the hard stuff of the working world, he adorned it with gold, accenting every decorative detail until the little space inhabited by the angel and the virgin became filled with the richness of divine mystery, a glowing casket like the briefcase in *Pulp Fiction*.

But, like the *Madonna del Parto*, the Cavalcanti *Annunciation* is marked by absence. Unlike most other treatments of Mary's encounter with Gabriel, Donatello's has no Holy Spirit in it, no Hand of God, no dove descending to the Virgin, no piercing ray to impregnate her. For all the richness of divine presence implied in its burnished gold and stately graciousness, it is as if The Divine is present only by reflection. The world is filled with God's glory, but God himself is nowhere to be seen. Having arrived, he's biding his time. He needs to be found.

The work in this book needs to be found too, to be paid attention before it will fully give itself up. Introducing Loydell's *Ballads of the Alone*, H.L. Hix discussed the 'difficulty' of his writing, the resistance it offers to the very conventions that it employs. The poems and prose in *Dear Mary* are similarly difficult, allusive and elusive, ekphrastic without strictly describing. Opposed to the facile, as Hix has it, they 'give form to invisible process'. However, what characterises them more than the form they give it is the space they leave for invisible process to work.

This space is sometimes literal. The opening thought of 'Displacement' is not about the recreated worlds of the Boyle Family's square metres of territory but about 'The holes in the map […] left by the darts we threw'. The 'segments of the world moved somewhere else' seem then not to be the Boyles' facsimiles but the places themselves, and the holes not indicators of what and where should be represented but markers of the places where a gap has been left in the world. The hiddenness of the Holy Spirit in Donatello's *Annunciation* has an echo in Loydell's 'Annunciations' with their 'Empty

---

[2] In the *Decameron*, in Elissa's tale of the foolish painter Calandrino, the trickster Maso del Saggio attempts to gull him into believing that it possesses special value, describing, 'due maniere di pietre […] di grandisssima vertú. L'una sono i macigni da Settignano'. Giovanni Boccaccio, *Tutte le opere di Giovanni Boccaccio: vol. IV, Decameron*, ed. Vittore Branca (Milan, 1965), Giornata 8, Novella 3, line 19, p. 683.

rooms / full of absence / waiting for / a child to arrive // and fill the world'. The child is coming, he is even conceived, but for now his absence is real.

But the absences from Loydell's work are not just those of missing objects – the Boyles' stolen square metre, Mary's child, the elusive representation of the Holy Spirit – or missing words. They are the spaces between ideas, which require the reader to engage off the page with whatever it might be that will fill the lacunae, completing not the sentence but the thought.

There is a riddling quality to Loydell's willingness to leave gaps in telling that has common cause with the images he engages with and (sometimes, somehow) describes. In them, the attempt to make mystery on the one hand and the impossibility of avoiding mystery on the other underlines the difficulty of any kind of ekphrasis, of the picture that records the world or the word that records the picture.

Thus 'What It Is': 'it is trying to look at strange photos / and guess what they are.' Loydell repeatedly insists on the inability of images to describe the world, and in particular its interaction with the numinous, any more successfully than words can. No kind of image or image capture is adequate to the task of making any clearer those things that are fundamentally beyond understanding. In 'Surveillance System Annunciation', there is 'Not much to go on. Here, look at the tape: / Something arrives, looking grey and blurred, / something too fast for our cameras to see, / something we can't identify.'

Equally, though, he dwells in 'Something More' on the equivalent incapacity of the word alone to express the Word. 'Attempting to create / an image of the Absolute / he decided to escape / the cage of language'. The escape is necessary. In 'Between', 'Words cannot accurately describe / the experience of light and tone, / the incremental changes and shifts / in between black and white'. Neither the verbal nor the visual can shoulder the burden alone and so it is in the movement back and forth between the two and in their repeated, complementary and contradictory efforts to give comprehensible form to the ineffable that the writing finds its rhythm.

What Loydell brings to the book as both writer and painter is the recognition that it is only the constituent parts of text and image, line, tone and hue, shifting and recombining, which are sufficiently agile to capture the fugitive picture. Sometimes it is necessary to 'rely only on paint / let colour do the talking'. Sometimes monochrome nouns are better for making images out of fragments, as in 'Ideas of Flight': 'The owl man has gone / away for winter; / leaving only memory, / talon, beak and eye.'

Georges Didi-Huberman, writing about Piero's near contemporary Fra Angelico, came to focus not on the lapidary clarity of his draughtsmanship or the sumptuous freshness of his colours, but on the fugitive dots and splotches of paint which pepper some of his frescoes at the Dominican convent of San Marco in Florence and in particular on the fictive marble panels beneath the *Madonna of the Shadows* in the dormitory corridor.[3] Alexander Nagel, reviewing Didi-Huberman, identifies the painter's aim in apparently having flicked and thrown paint randomly across his otherwise immaculate picture as being to produce, 'something like a performative analogue to the mysterious process by which the divine "seed" is disseminated in all things'.[4] For Nagel, 'the point of Didi Huberman's analysis is not to reveal what the panels "signify" unequivocally.... He is instead interested in how they participate in a plurivocal "figural" economy in which meaning is relayed from figure to figure and from place to place without taking on substance, producing something like a cloud of associations that "circle endlessly around a mystery".'[5]

Here, though, a cloud is too imprecise and too fugitive a vehicle for the conveyance of meaning. The 'cage of language' is a necessary confinement. This is a book of words, after all, a linguistic rather than a performative analogue to the problem of representing the unrepresentable, whose poems pick at its lock to reveal (without ever actually showing) that the elusiveness of grace is not the same as its absence. If there is a lesson here (and, of course, there need not be but Loydell is also a teacher) it is in the tension between the various kinds of absence and presence that these poems paradoxically embody. The invisibility of the incarnation is not the same as its withholding. The world is not empty of the divine, but pregnant with it, suffused by it. Mary is not alone and neither are we.

Dr. Jim Harris
Andrew W Mellon Foundation Teaching Curator
Ashmolean Museum of Art and Archaeology
University of Oxford

---

[3] Georges Didi-Huberman, *Fra Angelico: Dissemblance and Figuration*, trans. Jane Marie Todd (Chicago, 1995).
[4] Alexander Nagel, 'Review of Recent Literature on Fra Angelico', *Art Bulletin*, vol.78, no.3, Sept 1996, pp.559-565, pp. 561-2.
[5] Ibid, p.561.

Dear Mary

'Dear Mary
Thank you for the day
We shared together'
    —Steve Miller, 'Dear Mary'

'Language and diagrams enable us to navigate the extra-ordinary complex terrain of colour and to communicate with one another about colour, and without them we would easily get lost. But at the same time there is a value in getting lost, in becoming immersed in the endless proliferation of natural blues or greens or yellows and greys that are always around us and always merging into one another, but which often go unnoticed.'
  —David Batchelor, *The Luminous and the Grey*

'The only thing that is different from one time to another is what is seen and what is seen depends on how everybody is doing everything. This makes the thing we are looking at very different and this makes what those who describe it make of it, it makes a composition, it confuses, it shows, it is, it looks, it likes it as it is, and this makes what is seen as it is seen.'
  —Gertrude Stein, 'Composition as Explanation'

Stop Looking

When you stop looking
the colours soften and blur.

Greens and blues become fog,
ochres and reds a stone block.

I can't tell if the sky is purple
or blue, deep orange or grey.

Everything is the colour of sun,
of dusty land; Tuscan memory.

Forecast

Viking   Fisher   Dogger
Disruption to travel and the possibility of fog,
maybe some apparitions or visitations.
But do not be afraid.

Rockall   Shannon   Malin
Temperature increasing, so no likelihood
of frost, but miracles and signs may occur.
Listen to what's being said.

Fastnet   Lundy   Sole
Bright lights and wings near Bethlehem
and reports coming in of voices,
along with shock and awe.

Fisher   Humber   German Bight
A cold front to follow, with the realisation
of what's happened. Things will be
unsettled in the coming weeks.

Gabriel   Mary   Joseph   John
The voice of one crying in the wilderness:
make straight in the desert a highway for our God.
Prepare ye the way of the Lord.

'A Process of Discovery'

for David Miller

'My writing must also, along
what unfamiliar way,
be company?'
  – David Miller, 'Unity'

The poet's book is one of the four I have brought away on holiday. It was a choice between my favourite versions of the short narrative poems of a Greek author, made especially awkward by the translator, who does not appear to be fluent in English, and my friend's new book.

Eventually, I decided on the poet's new collected poems, and looked forward to the dislocation between warm Tuscan light and the nameless grey cities that often form a background to his fragmented texts.

With shutters pinned back, windows wide, sun burning through morning cloud, the poems speak of love, confusion, moments and ideas, all threaded into necklaces of language.

•

The colours in my set of paints never match the colours outside. I have to work hard to find the muted tones of mist or dusk, even more to mix the faded earths and stones, the burnt greens that fill the view.

I have little need for red – a few roof tiles here and there, and only use yellow to mix variations of foliage in the distance. Neither the earth nor stone seem at all brown, more grey and off-white. The distant mountains require blue to give them distance, purples and greys if the light has gone or a storm arrived.

•

There is hardly any music here.

Sometimes a faint radio
in the distance,
a few CDs in our hire car
for long journeys,

those drummers we watched
at a medieval fair –
the whole village play acting
for a weekend.

A falcon flew
off into the silence.
A saxophone,
a clarinet:

reported
conversations
on the pages
of his book.

•

Despite itself,
the silence
is the event,

the appearance
of the angel
is the event,

the moment
as pregnant
as the madonna;

bird spirit
of God
top right,

a sparrow
flying across
window-framed sky.

•

In one version the angel
speaks in painted script,

is always speaking,
never silent.

I prefer the mute
gold wings of flight,

the ethereal earth
beneath celestial feet,

the always unsaid
unbelievable truth.

•

The poet's book has served me well, and has sat literally and
conceptually alongside a short book on colour, a re-read novel
of occult training and enlightenment, and a fictional exploration
of moments when the celestial and human met or even touched.

Our conversation has been a long one. We first met on the page
and later in the flesh, but there is still a lot to be said.

For the moment, I am again listening.

•

The sun is even brighter now.

It is clear my painting's colours are all wrong.

I rinse my brushes and head out for a swim.

A startled lizard runs from the sudden splash.

Lost in Colour

Phil who I knew at college
used to say that I was
seduced by colour, which
he meant as a criticism
but I thought was great.

Oh how my paintings sang,
how the edges zinged.
You could stain and pour,
risk everything each time
you touched a canvas.

But nature is always
greater than the sum of
my parts: oil on water,
sunset over the creek,
mist on morning hills…

It's important not to
compare yourself with god
or others, or hope to
best the world outside.
Now I'm reduced

to black and white:
shadows on the page,
cold lines of type,
pale marks and
faint grey stains.

Lost in colour,
I don't have
the words
although words
are all I have.

Three Circles in a Row

My hat's been on all day.

I made the purple more blue,
have spent a lifetime learning to feel nothing.

I find it's almost never the same.

I swallow my pride, start with goodbye;
there is a long time before anything happens.

Welcome: please arrive before you depart.

Faint bird tracks in the snow.

Annunciations

Empty rooms
behind the madonna
as the angel
gives his news.

Empty rooms
in perspective,
their vanishing points
all vanished.

Empty rooms
filled with light,
Mary's stool or throne
always outside.

Empty rooms
full of absence,
waiting for
a child to arrive

and fill the world.

The Pictures Started to Instruct Me

1. All the Colours

I wanted all the colours to be present at once.
(Our chromatic decisions are not fully rational.)

How difficult it becomes when one
tries to get very close to the facts:

various intensification and dilutions take place,
colour is still only a beginning.

2. Monochromatic Triads

The important thing here is
a slow dance of golden lights,
the transformation of structure.

I put down my magnifying glass;
a world without colours
appears to us dead.

3. The Process

All of this is highly speculative;
there is no logical argument.

AVOID THE SYMBOLIC
AVOID THE IMAGINATIVE

Otherwise it would still be
a representation of light,

a large and expanding collage
fleeing extinction through a meadow.

4. Colour Exceeds the Word

Colour is pure thought.
Colour is a vast problem.

Intelligent beings have a language
I will not attempt to describe.

Colour has its own meaning.

Colour by Numbers

Colour by number pages
are a fun way for everyone
to learn their colours and numbers.

I've had quite a few people
ask me if I would be
making a work of art.

Find the correct answer
and you'll have new ideas
for a fresh and funky look.

•

Colouring is always fun and you can take it to the next level:
log in now to enhance and personalize your experience!
Download this lovely colouring-in page for your little ones.

Every picture is available in three modes:
easy, difficult, and spring's famous cherry blossoms:
colours that drift the length of the forest.

•

Match the colours to the key to reveal
all sorts of pictures and patterns,
from parrots hiding amongst the leaves
to a gaggle of monsters and a city scene.

By working different sequences of moves
it is possible to create different structures,
enforcing both colour compatibility
and generous spatial arrangements.

Computers store drawings, photographs
and other pictures using only numbers.
Did you know that all the colours you see
are represented by hexadecimal code?

The following activity demonstrates
how they can do this. Find out.
We are the collective effort,
a uniquely talented creative team.

Cimabue

Memory makes a noise
like paint peeling,
dark flood water
falling away.

Death by drowning:
the ruined crucifix
still floats in imagination,
resurrected and restored.

Flakes of reverence
and moments of dusk;
everything in Italy
is a love letter to God.

Hidden

I am wondering if
the annunciation angel
will speak to me today,
or be silent in the museum;
silenced even.

How does paint speak
down the centuries,
flaking from a forgotten wall
or crumbling in a shadowed chapel,
overlooked by tourists and guides?

There are hidden angels
everywhere in Tuscany.
If you find one keep quiet
and speak of it only to yourself,
let meaning turn to whisper.

Assisi

We drove over to see the angel. Made our pilgrimage across the plain, leaving the fast dual carriageway intent on going somewhere else for the Roman road which heads directly to the hill town.

From a distance the monastery monumental at the village's end; the fortress at the top of another hill; the cathedral dwarfing its surround.

At the back of the museum, a small annunciation (artist unknown) and a wooden madonna & child, weathered into abstraction since the 12th century.

Why are these things hidden away, waiting to be seen? We were the only visitors to the museum that afternoon.

Ice cream in the square. One afternoon the temperature 41° C outside the car. The air-conditioning struggling, our child sleeps fitfully.

We put you on the train to go home; later, we will drive ourselves to the airport.

There is a small wasps' nest in a clumsy stone sculpture at the end of the track near where we stayed.

We are hoping to take the room on tour, might one day learn to swim in the presence of the Other.

In the Dark, Listening Carefully

for David Toop

The cicadas and motorway drone
are always there, and sometimes
a cough across the valley or a car
on a rough track is foregrounded.
What we see or hear is difficult to place;
fading light brings the hills nearer,
evening mist pushes them to the horizon.

David Toop writes about paintings
containing sound: they are not silent
as we once thought. Frozen movement
implies captured noise, implies
speech and conversation always
underway, the push and pull of
language alive and overheard.

I haven't written, drawn or painted
a thing. Just watched and listened.
We didn't get to see the angel.
Although the signs said open
and entrance lights were on,
the glass door refused to move,
the interior remained unlit.

I have a memory of gold
and rose-pink robes, outspread
wings and Mary's coy surprise.
Last year Fra Angelico's annunciation
lay in bubblewrap on the floor,
this summer it's still silenced,
message hidden out of sight.

Tonight

Tonight, I watched the moon move
from left to right above blue hills.

White in the midday sky,
it now glows cream in the dark.

The air bruises through purple
to charcoal to ultramarine.

My candle scares the insects away,
flickers and smokes as it gives out

almost enough light to read by
until poems blur and I abandon text

for evening sky. I cannot read the stars,
prefer the morse of distant cars,

village streetlights shimmering in the heat,
a bat's leather flit across the darkened valley.

Out of Bounds

Distant hills
move closer
as the light fades.
Greys take over
mid-afternoon.

There is already
a chorus of cicadas
calling to cars
heard long before
and long after
they pass by.

Another church,
whose frescoes
I wanted to see,
is closed for repairs,
its overgrown garden
out of bounds
behind locked gates.

Between

after David Batchelor

He writes of grey, of greys,
and how we cannot define them,
only compare and contrast
more than one, to see if
they are warmer or colder,
contain more green or red.

Grey, he quotes, *is never luminous*:
we have names for only a few
of the thousands of colours
around us. We improvise and
negotiate, compare and group,
neatly divide the spectrum up

using manageable language.
Words cannot accurately describe
the experience of light and tone,
the incremental changes and shifts
in between black and white,
the greys between this grey and that.

Almost Angel

'I just wanted to paint a white and grey picture
that would still have colour in its veins
as we have blood under our winter-white skin'
    —Dorothea Tanning, re. *A Mi-Voix*, 1958

Spinning dervish of paint,
yellow leaking through.
Abstract notes for new maps;
we're at home in fairyland.

A man scratches his head
at a *trompe l'oeil* room
painted on the walls of
the room he has just entered.

A pub where the market
runs out, where the day
turns into night, without
shopping for dusk.

We was brought up here
and was happy for a while.
Almost angel: different
dimensions and identities.

Fra Angelico's Pronunciation

for Jessica, whose phrase it was

Because the painter
always lisped
so did the angel,
and Mary when nervous
had a bit of a stutter.

It was an awkward moment,
but we forget the details
and let ourselves be dazzled
by Gabriel's painted wings,
the pinks and blues and gold.

Alone and in shock
after hearing his message,
Mary tries to still herself,
to p-p-p-onder these things
in her hea-ar-ar-art-t-t.

Stuttering

'I've often argued that colour is
a kind of embarrassment to language.'
  —David Batchelor

Small areas of colour
spill from behind black.

I'm not sure if it's a blood clot
or scab, or what the difference is.

Turns out he wrote the book
about stuttering which I'd read,

as well as the book of quotes
and ideas that I love.

Poured paint's allowed to buckle
and scar as it dries out:

small pools of colour
above black on the page.

Rain in Tuscany

It never rains in Tuscany
in July, but it is raining
so much today that streams
are flowing down the street
outside the restaurant as
bruised mustard clouds
block the head of the valley.
It is the wettest rain ever,
which takes forever to fall,
slowly explodes upon impact
and lasciviously soaks
into and through everything
that it touches and finds
except for the stone pavement
which glistens then shines,
divests itself of the downpour,
diverts it elsewhere: new runnels
and rivulets, rivers and streams,
all finding their way down
to the bottom of whichever road
they are on, as heavyweight sky
slowly makes way for new sun.
It never rains in Tuscany.

How to Say It

He does not know how to say it,
how to talk about the moment
he has been asked to paint,

so he simply colours the story in:
blue here, pink there, crimson, gold…
Struggles to show heaven's light,

keeps coming back to the quiet girl,
who is somewhat bemused
by the angel in overdrive

making such a fuss
about a surprise pregnancy
and how her child will save the world.

Through a Glass Darkly

Scraping away the layers,
old varnish gone brown,
the painting turned out
to be an annunciation,
Mary and an angel
facing each other down.

Small butterfly wings
spreading from his back
put Mary's blue dress
to shame. The colours
of heaven illumine and
transform the world,

a prophetic rainbow
that self-declares
this is the moment
the world's waited for,
a conversation worth
capturing in paint.

Over-Spoken

from/for David Hart

Form matters: yourpoemsgotoofast

I find myself   splitting
               lines,

spreading
        phrases
               out,

  opening   up   spaces

   and
        moving the language

  out
     of
     essay
     form

into something

        that

   can
          breathe

     more

        freely

 and allow time

for proper listening (her voice)

  and sensing presence

      (which then flies off)

Taken

after Deborah Turbeville

I make stories out of colours
I don't own, trinkets I have
collected wherever I go.

If you stay too long
people suspect you
and question your presence.

I slip in and out of shadows
to find beautiful objects
I would like to own
then take them.

The queen of heaven
is scratched and burnt
and her courtiers
live in a cardboard box.

Tape your memories
to the wall and let me
photograph them.
Then take them.

The devil says
it is all very difficult,
there must be an easier way
to show who is in charge.

Dusk arrives, cold stars shine,
imaginary chairs settle
and creak in the night.
A church bell chimes.

These might be
your memories.
Let me take them.

Past Imperfect

after Deborah Turbeville

Bleached digital scans;
yesterday's fashion shoots
in a new picture book.

Veils and lace, mascara,
sandpapered sketchbooks,
out-of-focus photos remastered.

The story goes like this:
once upon a time there was a glass house
and beautiful women all threw stones…

The story used to go like this:
once there was an abandoned bath house
haunted by fashion-shoot ghosts…

Or it might have gone like this:
two brothers lived alone in a big house
with only each other for company…

It is yesterday and tomorrow
we will all find ourselves
living in the past imperfect,

in an empty town at the end of the story,
in the far corners of the unknown where
everything is magic, always slightly blurred.

Taken Up

It is the loveliest of mornings.
Life in the here and now begins
with some sort of visitation
and the desire for affirmation,

the idea of a well-defined reward
in heaven. Taking our cue from
the liquid interchangeability
of colour and light, we note

that Mary is so taken up with God
she fails to notice the muscular
young man hovering in her room.
By focussing on the inner life

she has missed the moment,
an opportunity for transcendence.
Her heaven may be imaginative
rather than something literal,

her annunciation not historical
but cultural, a folded paper note
passed along the back row of class
under the eyes of Joseph and God.

The mouth of the imaginary angel
is closed; the human body is a house,
open to the world around; heaven
a product of communal desire.

Online Dating Annunciation

He arrived unseen, almost as though he had flown in through the window. He was taller and better looking than I'd expected and kept his back turned away from me. There was a luminosity about him, or perhaps it was just his strange bright clothes. He was very attractive, anyway, though different from the photo on his profile.

He went to speak, but I put my finger on his lips and let my robes fall open. Smiled encouragingly and beckoned him to follow me. He told me not to be afraid, and I laughed and said I wasn't, that Joseph wouldn't be home for hours. Did he like what he saw?

When he disrobed, it was a bit of a shock to see what he'd kept hidden. He folded his wings around me and we made love all afternoon. I've never been so fulfilled, so satisfied. It was heavenly. Then he departed from me.

What an angel! I long to see him again.

Lives of the Saints

after Michael Landy

legs, arms and
oops a daisy

spring in her step
(spring is her step)

secondhand assortment
rodded limbs

back to base
weighed right down

head full of gears
central heating discord

broken futures
partially assembled

all fingers and thumbs
iron angle signs

•

what is real
sixth sense vibration
no resistance

a life of penance
plastercast body burn
self-battering belief

faith in splinters
torture devices
ideas and imagery

listening to
another world
outside the door

for the moment
up front positive
canonised clone

mishaps, misshapen
and bad timing
failure admitted

more than one finger
denial of self
well, yes and no

•

the sound of the bell
glass room procession

people as images
scrapyard connect

we used to dance
father forgive

•

he began by
entering the building

breaking things
and winding himself up

losing interest
for the sake of it

trying to imply
ascension

Annunciation by Francis Bacon

Imagine! His smudges of raw paint
pulled into communion with the past:

the angel ill-defined, contorted,
with a gash for a mouth, can hardly

speak to the flesh wound that is
Mary's face. Instead of a portico

and private cell there's a room
outlined against saturated colour.

The dove is either that splash there
or has gone missing altogether.

You should be afraid. Should scream
and slur your speech, get drunk.

The spirit of God is upon you,
urgent and toxic. You're soused,

unable to speak or think, have
been winging it from the word go.

Shadow Triptych

after Francis Bacon

The Dissolution of Self into the Shadow

Ragged young women with wild long hair peer at a voluptuous sprawl of paint. All smear and smudge at optimum distance, splash and line up close, full of crises and abrupt shifts, a scarecrow is pinned to the bed with questionable symbols. Heavy black heels clump away, allowing a process of mythification to continue. Utopia is at a new stage in development, our traditions are continually renewable expressions of life. It is very agreeable to dissolve back into the realm from which your professional discipline has exiled you.

In the corner a skinny old man in a raincoat tries to find a shadow to hide in. He seems to be forced down by the light. He is learning that balance need not direct us to give equal weight to what must be weighted differently. The corners are too bright, engaging architectural constructs at their weakest point. He stands alone, shocked by the energy of paint, frightened by staring eyes framing a blur of movement, by the way the paintings refuse to follow him round the room. Sight is no longer the sense that constitutes the subject. Perception is closely linked to eternity in the moment.

The sea is a field. In the field there is a bed. The bed is a ship, and on the bed the captain is naked. He is violently turning under the artist's hand and the viewer's eye. It is easier to mend relationships than talk about the repression of female form in representational art. Men must keep their distance: a cultural fabrication stuck in a border position, free to be responsible people. They must assume familiar imagery in order to make themselves known. How many exhibitions contain true images which will solve all our problems? How many shows are overhung and under-curated, containing the merely orthodox?

In the dark doorway the skull of the artist shines in greysilver paint. He is the lost self incarnated. His hair is cut, he is put into masculine dress, he must concern himself with war. A smudge would wipe him away like charcoal. We make connections in a hotchpotch manner, which on the face of it have little or no reason. Thus we recognise the concerns raised: the blurring of gender, the loss of self, transformation into shattered fragments. A state of serene and apparently unending bliss follows. We need not decide for ourselves in what directions we should travel.

The artist does not know what to say, but enjoys saying it nonetheless. The question of madness runs right through. Purple and red, the viridian moves focus to another bed, another nailed corpse. Breaking down information is far more interesting than ritual gesture. Holding fast to doubt means the left hand branch breaks, the rattlesnake travels around your head. Whatever that is supposed to be, could it be capable of fixing something so delicate? What counts may be what we do with the future.

Step into the shower through smeared stripes of curtain, and shout at yourself being crucified. The world is violent orange. A dancer hangs lifeless from a beam, a chimp squats in the grass. The Pope blesses us from his cartoon armchair. Now we are holy. Life consists of countless do's and don'ts, but I am troubled by what you mean by poetry. The medium is no longer the goal, we eroticize the things that fill us with horror. Rational cognition confidently moves us toward change, fusion made synthetic.

In the corner a man on a red sofa scratches at the air, revealing the links between power, metaphysics, theological realism and visual pleasure. We can see right through elaborate ideology to the painter's mark. I began with wry observation and distance, but now experience harmonisation and reconciliation: we are marked right through by the painter. Deep space sucks the soul dry, religious experience installs itself in the heart, clad in the most imaginatively potent vocabulary currently available, interspersed with sad stories. But is there any need to focus on the word?

The scarecrow lolls on the box, liquid shadow flowing toward the gallery floor. A strange reversal has been working itself out: gold is no longer gold, for it has become light. It came within three feet of my foot as I sat on the red sofa, hand cupping my ear. Maybe it was all angel – it's been with me longer than painting has. Art has become both impossible and easy; I think that I've been influenced. Everything is simultaneously interconnected, except in periods clouded over by frivolity or utopia.

Danger darkens the stranger's home. A right-angle line holds him in the corner; he cannot move. His shoes are only vague outline, his habitat has only been quickly chalked in. Yet, what is conceived in isolation endures, a sort of echo from one artist to another. I have turned all my practical difficulties into theoretical ones. A state of unending bliss, the dream of immortality, would seem to be realisable, but I am troubled by what you mean by poetry. Dynamism began with the Fall. We fell asleep at once.

Tears of blood, trails of paint. If we see things black it is because we weigh them in the dark: the light dying within a gold frame, the light reflected in the glass. We eroticize horror that makes us full of things and manage to forget that we are the guilty parties. The young are not very talented, there has been no substantial change that makes our world different from previous worlds. We should have dispensed with evolution and practised our drawing. By losing contact with words we lose contact with human beings.

A shadow tries to find a raincoat to hide in. It passes very quickly, with not a moment's hesitation. Plenty of painters are immersed in images in such a way that concepts always appear to be figurative. When your image appeared, developing in that astonishing way, it was a remarkable moment. I find comfort, hope even, in the fact that knowledge cannot get inside my skin. I do not have an orderly mind and am never afraid to leap into the dark. Here we are, both convinced of the importance of the problem of explanation. We no longer need to talk of perfection, intelligence has never made great art.

Tread the bed with bare hands, avoiding the corpse spread out across your duvet. The slatted blind is crimson in the centre of the window. If human blood can be contaminated, what is to prevent the global economy from contracting a deadly virus? Images are addictive; the remedy must be stronger than the disease. The future is noise and machines and crowds and confusion. One realises why both meditation and action require silence. I was right to come out to the woodshed. I invite everyone to stand in front of the door I have closed in their face.

Weary, eyes veiled with madness, people tell me the compatibility problem is still not solved; but if you see the newspapers you can't help but be aware of what goes on. I read for the shipwrecked feeling I get, to trudge down a road growing darker and darker. What a wonderful thing, to keep quiet and live without motives; to stretch out between two graves. Painting is so fluid that one can't note anything down. What is important is the clearing of the way for contact with dreams. We need an economy of image, a mixture of enthusiasm and the unexpected.

The task that remains is to learn to have a lapse of memory and wipe the past away like charcoal. The most important thing is to look at the painting in a gutter rather than on a pedestal. The medium invites a spontaneous, sketchy approach. I have always sought out landscapes that preceded realism: the dawn of spring with the woods near at hand; an unexpected patch of green meadow; the clear, cool morning shining in greysilver paint. What I seek is simply being: here is the rain, here is silence, here the pool of water after the storm. Try to react much more in front of an image than when listening to sounds; try to put light under your mattress.

The bell tolls, the floor is heaped with boxes. We apprehend objects by wrapping them up in language: light-weight components easily assembled by unskilled men. Workers clump away into the corner of the artist's mind, don goggles and gloves. I remember them in the cellar, violently exploring the idea of energy. Critical realists are not particularly concerned with paint: art has become impossible, utopia has departed for a secret destination. Words bring us to life and make our world. It is time for afternoon tea; the day holds up its hands.

I listen with astonishment and sleep with the autumn wind. I stretch full out on the grass and kick off my shoes. There seems no end to the shades of green. This meadow, an area largely unknown to tourists, is an ideal area for transformation; we can confidently make moves for change. The world is there to be constructed. I cannot help my lapses of memory, transience requires constantly expanding networks. My every word is linked to endless chains of reference, designed to respond to the needs of the traffic; essential tools for anyone in the arts.

The captain dragged me to where the stars, isolated from everyday public life, voice sorrow. A skinny stranger stood alone, not knowing what to say. Party to guilt, we became disappointed by the various forces bearing upon us; the natural and unnatural impossibly confused in a shipwreck of feeling. It was a remarkable moment. Great drumbeats of time could supply water to the age of cinema, which in turn encourages cycling and walking rather than painting. We believe we are making beautiful things, primarily visual objects.

He told me of nights alone, hearing footsteps like cymbals, of compact neighbourhoods and over-grown gardens, of providence at work – an occult force pinned to the bed. I did not know what to say, yet recognised the concerns raised. Framed by the most imaginatively potent curtains the world seems to become a beautiful domed room. Through radio and television, I try to keep in step with change. I find myself disagreeing very strongly with key ideas, simply because of my simple nature.

Dark and cunning, language and the world have become shifting and fluid; a pool of water smudged by a passing storm. The compatibility problem is still not solved: I am troubled by what you mean by poetry, you turn your back on companionship and the sun. Preservation is obviously preferable to unchanging divine love; men must keep their distance. Patterns of light move on the ceiling and edge along the walls; they engage the passers-by deciding in which direction they must travel. Shadows refuse to follow me, fall silent and progressively fade away in the overgrown garden to which there is no end.

I awake in the corner of the room, re-shaped, redecorated, replumbed and relit. I don't have either a fixed position or a fixed identity, I did not choose this wallpaper or the form of the city. Night after night the process of creation flows through us, leaping in the dark, not particularly real. We judge for ourselves the way we respond to noise and confusion; painting is so fluid within and beyond the walls of the academy. For me it is a problem to get any serious writing done at any time, the door is often closed in my face. To attempt to re-open the book is to spark the imagination and move the spirit; each of us has to disguise our own voice.

Darkness soaks me like a fever. We are history and I do not know what to say or how to draw. Nothing prepared me for what I saw that night. Horror is becoming more streamlined and elaborate, it has made it difficult for us to see. Orthodox subjection cannot enter my mind. Through skilful advertising, a process of mythification continues: timeless news about timeless objects. Would it be possible for a revolution to occur? Have you got on the train? How many true images adopt a certain starting point? Will figurative images solve all our problems? Aren't we really rather marvellous ourselves? I'll slip out quietly for now.

An Open Secret

The valley is full of milk this morning:
fog poured into every nook and cranny.

There are pink flowers here, and there,
and layers of soupy greens and grey
gradually evaporating in the pale sun.

The distance is still unknown,
sky and land's meeting an open secret
that cannot be seen.

I can draw the horizon anywhere
and mix greys to cover up the page,
everything I cannot see.

There is no wind. No sun. No view.

The House Over There

'How do I draw the house over there?'
asks my daughter, exasperated.
I show her in my notebook,
but apparently I've got it wrong –
that is not what she can see.

Things continue to stay as they were,
to haunt us, chase after us,
into holidays and dreams. Alone
in the morning mist, small voices
distract, as does music in the distance.

The coffee machine splutters,
somebody out of sight coughs,
and I keep looking, have just noticed
another building that has never appeared
in my paintings but will always have to now.

Alien Annunciation

UFOs, paranormal activities, vortexes, underground alien bases, alien races, alien encounters and apportations are just some of the issues you will find in this poem. A boomerang-shaped object seen from an airport and a woman's encounter with an angel are among the secrets revealed.

Please share your UFO experiences and beliefs and discuss the conceptual and evolutionary implications of near-death experiences and UFO encounters as shamanic initiations. Several pilots have come forward over the years to talk about their experiences, each of them searching for esoteric secrets.

I was taken by aliens! I saw a disc-shaped craft land vertically on my farm, and when the hatch opened unexplained lights in the forest turned out to be angels and aliens from another dimension. The UFO was real and solid, because it was picked up by tracking radar, but nobody has talked.

One of the most fascinating and strategic topics in ancient texts is the record of fallen angels, giants, and UFOs. It's not uncommon for animals to act in an agitated manner during UFO encounters, and according to Mary her pet's barking continued to get louder and louder throughout the visitation. Then the angel departed from her.

Ranking as one of the most famous paranormal incidents in history – and now a pop culture phenomenon, the angel Gabriel was sent by God to a town in Galilee. Something passed underneath us, quite close, and became a reflection on the nature of language. Impossible things happened, but the angel retained his mystic aura, particularly in the steamy androgyny he bought to his performance. This would provide a template for a new kind of occult imagining.

Mary uncovered various pictures and transcripts of astronaut conversations from space missions that related to encounters with angels. The local military commander (quite alarmed by such encounters) decided to capture one of the creatures. Mary later had several odd psychic experiences and further encounters. A lot of this had to do with the initial drive to sell the brand.

The UFO landed near Joseph's workplace, and two figures exited the ship to explain the strange science behind the virgin birth. Avid watchers of the skies celebrate World UFO day. It's no coincidence that so many people who encounter UFOs really want to believe in them, but that doesn't explain the term 'High Strangeness' which refers to the concept of secret identities hidden behind masks and make-up.

What is the psychospiritual significance of the UFO phenomenon? UFO sightings movies reflect the common fascination of people with other beings from distant planets visiting the earth but are definitely antithetical to orthodox Christian belief. Helicopters are used for psychological intimidation, surveillance of the individuals associated with UFO encounters, those looking for angels.

To conclude, the doctrine of the eternal generation of the Son, understood as involving the communication of the divine essence, is not only the historic position of the church, but it is a biblical doctrine essential to an orthodox formulation of UFO encounters, often with a dark tinge but dressed up in cosmic finery. For nothing is impossible with God.

The Dark Figure

Dazzling light. The dark figure
mentioned earlier dives back
into the fire. As a gesture,
it has great impact, offering
both tragedy and divine comedy.

Heaven is revealed to us
in a mystical flash or vision,
colours find their counterparts,
questions jump towards God
and what were once answers

are now just fading superstition.
Until the dawn of the century
the interior and external journey
was one and the same, but then
imagination twisted eternity

and our historical world of time
together. The priests insisted
upon resurrection, offering
affirmation of the impossible
with tea and biscuits after.

An emphasis on precision
and detail means we must
take several steps away from
the picture, towards impending
doom. We can all make choices

about the end of the world
and use psychological insight
with regard to the self and
the next stage of the journey.
Death is not a happy reunion.

How Grey Became

The colour grey is preferred by people who are indecisive;
grey is also the colour of evasion and non-commitment.
Grey is an unemotional colour, shields us from outside influence.

Grey is a sophisticated colour which gives a clean graphic look.
Look for the colour in grey and the grey in colour:
grey paint gives interior walls and ceilings a popular matt finish.

Grey is the colour of intellect, knowledge, and wisdom,
the only colour that has no direct psychological properties.
The world of adults is grey; grey walls make a dramatic statement.

Grey colours can be used to create a very sophisticated paint scheme.
Despite being cool in colour, greys are capable of adding drama.
The colour grey offers a nice touch of sophistication.

Welcome to the grey week of Team Inspiration's Colour School.
As promised, the recipe for perfect grey: individual horizons
should be defined when moist; use colour for its own sensual ends.

Just when you think you've checked all the shades of grey,
along comes a whole new paint collection.
Grey and gray are actually two different colours.

Adding grey paint to a paint of low to moderate chroma
(the visual grey we perceive when our eyes are closed)
means the same greyscale value diminishes the chroma.

Make friends with the colour grey, it offers natural camouflage.
Which colours work well with grey? Other greys or try a gray.
Grey's always been and always will be my preferred colour!

The Surreal House

1. Uniforms for the Dedicated

Impractical clothing that looks fantastic,
available in many different sizes and shapes.

It's exactly what it sounds like:
life that just makes you shake your head.

2. Stairs to Nowhere

Learn how to step
inside a labyrinth of chambers.

The signposts have all been repainted;
everywhere leads to somewhere nice.

This world is home to dry thunder
and streets covered in impassable layers of ice.

3. Corporate Relocation Specialists

The inspector was a rather intimidating guy
with a badge that hung around his neck.

He asked questions with a big stone heart,
preparing for a surge of content.

She was so surprised she forgot to tell him
she couldn't possibly go.

4. Real Time Storm Coverage

Forget fake rock overhangs, I like taking photos
in abandoned houses and forests.

I opened my eyes to memory
and saw the horizon approaching:

visual drift, assisted collapse,
near but far away.

Distance

The tree house in the woods
up on the mountain
becomes ordinary as you get nearer.

The magic is in the distance,
heat's shimmer and blur;
imagining what we don't know.

Silent Annunciation

The angel has nothing to say.

Within

Naum Gabo, Tate St Ives

Stroked into life,
figures dance
in the dome
of static electricity.

Enclosed spaces
enable the cube
to contain
the curves,

frame absences
within. 'Space
is the material
not the subject',

'Space should
participate in
the making of
a sculpture'.

You have
mathematics
in your head;
wood and wire.

Now cage the birds.

Ideas of Flight

The Conquest of the Air, Roland Penrose

The owl in my head
turns focus inward
and pecks away
my sense of self.

Thought is caged
by ideas of flight
that will never be.
My feathered friend

sleeps all day
and hunts at night;
I try to keep up
beneath the stars.

The owl man has gone
away for winter;
leaving only memory,
talon, beak and eye.

Dear Mary

Mary, you're covered in roses, in ashes,
you're covered in rain, and in babies.
In the morning you'll be alright,
in the morning the sun's gonna shine.

Emotions split from intellect, spirit split from flesh,
a joyful affirmation of the female in salvation.
She gave me a sign, she heard me pray,
let me know this dark night won't last always.

She said she'd call but that was weeks ago;
paradox is echoed in a new spiritual age.
A woman's body is to be celebrated
as central to nature transformed.

Were you ever in doubt?
Does it help to know you're not the only one?
This dark night won't last always,
nothing's quite as pretty as Mary in the morning.

I can live with the moods of Mary
if that's the way it has to be.
A child of confusion, she runs to the hills,
past the willows of illusion, trying not to cry.

Sweet Lady Mary has to rest her poor head
in a sacred place that is rooted in tradition.
Chasing the rainbow in her dreams so far away,
she wakes in the morning to breakfast in bed.

She speaks with the voice of an angel,
she smiles a heavenly smile,
with occasional hints of assertiveness
and the power of Mother Eve.

O Mary don't you weep and don't you mourn,
we are all divided creatures, fundamentally,
and I never lost one minute of sleepin'
worryin' 'bout how things might have been.

Lord, tell me the place women occupy
in creation and society.
I just brought these flowers for Mary,
I haven't seen Mary for years.

Her Room

after Andrew Wyeth

Her room turned inside out:
cold light shines in
and bright wind blows through;
one item remains on a trunk.

She has left and taken the sun,
taken the sky, all the trees.
Why did she leave this pale shell
I now hold to my ear?

Long shadows and dust,
ragged curtains faded to gauze;
do not breathe or step
any nearer. Absence makes

the heart grow fondue,
each memory now coated
in desire and hurt and loss.
How far away the sea.

Something More

Attempting to create
an image of the Absolute,
he decided to escape
the cage of language
and rely only on paint,
let colour do the talking.

There was a collision:
blue meets red and in-
between the implied space
of speech, annunciation.
Behind them the past
continuously rewinds

and we can never forget
we know all the stories
about Adam and Eve,
apples and snakes,
were all made
in the same image

but out of focus,
painted quickly
on wet plaster,
fading as we dried,
forgetting to forgive
or be forgiven.

His imagination
took flight and
angels appeared
when least expected,
shocking us to see
the troubling moment

when heaven interfered,
breaking its own rules,
and the world started again.
Everything is making you;
we were nothing anyway.
Hope is something more.

Displacement

(The Boyle Family)

The holes in the map are left by the darts
we threw at it to see where we would go.

We gathered up debris others had left
as they moved on or were asked to leave.

Four foot squares hung on the wall,
segments of world moved somewhere else:

yellow lines and tarmac, chewing gum and stones
embedded in the gravel. This poem resembles you,

it is short and all over the place. Then is still now,
although the frame is cracked in this happening space

and no-one talks about us any more. I found
an old book in the library, folded corners and

brown stains. That was then but we are still
looking for places and making marks on the map,

virtually there but with no memory, only pictures
on the hard drive and a burnt-up credit card

because we didn't know when to stop.
It won't be long before now and then converge,

before your far-reaching sense of context
can be reined-in and rewritten, managed and contained.

Out of the Picture

I never seem to be in the picture.
(Mind you, I wasn't there.)

I make it into nativity scenes
(I was the one found the stable),

but I'm never on the same canvas,
not even as supporting cast.

Adam and Eve leaving Eden,
the fiery angel throwing them out,

are often in the background;
God leans down from above

as a dove flies somewhere
between heaven and earth,

but mostly it's Mary and him,
some gaudy show-off angel

proclaiming and announcing,
telling my wife-to-be

what's going to happen next,
pre-empting our future together,

pushing me out of the picture
into eternity's disinterested gaze.

Where I Am

for Mark

Stop wagging your finger,
it won't do you any good.
I am trying to match
bookmarks to the books
I have decided to read.
I pick up freebies everywhere I go
and find myself with a collection,
it's always been that way,
but nothing suits this book of poems,
these essays about art,
and I worry about creasing
the cards I collected in New York
or my ticket from the museum in Italy
that houses my favourite painting ever.
The angel points his finger at Mary,
supposedly brings honour and joy,
but behind them Adam and Eve
flee the garden and someone
reframed this altarpiece
and slightly got it wrong.
The commemorative leather strip
of the moon landing might do
although it would be better if
you calmly told them you
were only parked from 9 at night
and that there is no reason for a fine.
Is Mary scared or delighted?
Take it on the chin like a man,
and pay up. Do not be afraid.
I have now read up to page 52
and used a scrap of paper
to mark exactly where I am.

Shake the Angel

Shake the angel.
Let his words fall
into the world.

Shake the words
like fruit from
golden branches.

Let the words fall
and be heard.
Let Mary hear.

Make the angel
come to his senses.
How can this be?

Shake the angel
and let his words fall
into memory,

let them hang
forever like fruit
on golden branches.

Surveillance System Annunciation

Not much to go on. Here, look at the tape:
Something arrives, looking grey and blurred,
something too fast for our cameras to see,
something we can't identify. Something
that startles the woman in the room.

She goes to get up, with a look of alarm,
but it appears that whatever-it-is
gestures at her to sit down again,
manages to calm her down although
what it then says is clearly surprising

as she seems totally lost for words,
But now the recording goes fuzzy
and by the time it clears again
there is only a woman sitting alone,
wondering what's just occurred.

My Paper Aunt

after Dorothea Tanning

My paper aunt dreams of luxury,
looks it up in five encyclopedias
before climbing the snowy stairs
to find out the truth about comets.

Under her table a shoal of fish
waits for food: on time off time,
whilst beyond the esplanade
there is only the blur of grey

that looks and feels like spray
on the face and mind. In dreams
she traps clouds in open shells;
stone totems surround her throne.

My paper aunt does not think
about the language of others,
preferring instead to avoid
any burden of sense or proof.

Madness is a chapter no medicine
can summarise; it is always
in search of a nervous system,
especially when it is time to play.

She often feels like dancing
in the invisible city she has built
outside this world but can never
open the door to walk out to.

My paper aunt paints portraits:
an exploded view will suffice
on the page if you go missing
as she turns you inside out.

The bereaved swan, the deathly
child, compositions in black:
these are shadows she omitted
between the roof and sky.

Bells are ringing in our ears,
but trains are for travelling
and defeating passport blues,
travel videos forever on repeat.

My paper aunt wants the evening
to be always. Everybody except her
knows this can not be true. It is true,
is a goodnight arrow into the dark.

She asks after Jane and Jane and Jane,
always asks for Jane and Jane and Jane;
demands they be found, rounded up
and fenced in. Nobody knows Jane

or can work our how to corral smoke.
Life smoulders and will not do anything
it is told; snow settles on the ground
as shooting stars freeze in the sky.

My paper aunt hates opera, plays it
all the time. She does not like
the sound it makes on the ceiling
or the green shirt modelled on the cover.

Her future is a collage of the past,
paint poured out and over, stroked
and swirled, seduced into shape.
She is both pronouncement and warning,

knows no more about the future than you
but is happy to oblige. She will follow
lines of enquiry off the edge of the page,
will arrive at yesterday any moment soon.

My paper aunt has never learnt to share,
cultivates unluck and a solemn stare.
There is enough lightning in her eyes
to feed a thousand storms; it will not

be long until some kind of ghost appears.
Sometimes the light plays tricks as
the day begins to return: fire walkers
in the clouds, glass and steel in the sky.

In her absence, you must measure
the length of the wind and weigh the owl
to the nearest feather. This everything
and nothing is one way to find out.

My paper aunt hopes to overcome depression
but the thought of it gets her down.
She does not want to talk about it,
instead asks us to look into ourselves

and turn what we see into maps.
Whilst no use for getting there,
information about the psychic terrain
is always useful; emotional geography

is a growing interest, she decides.
Information shifts the boundaries
and rules as she re-imagines home.
It is sometimes best to stay away.

My paper aunt lights the silent lamp
and waits for the tangled moment
to unravel. She is on the road to joy,
she says, and is learning to love

what we despise. Her argument
with time is the way that history
never reveals itself; it is dark
on the long journey to the light.

Outside, spring pushes winter aside
and hopes autumn will not arrive.
You cannot meet my aunt in person,
only repeat rumours and lies.

My paper aunt is out for a walk
and planning to visit herself.
Stories reach me via folk songs
and poems about the dead.

She is other, unlike no other,
sails everywhere in a day;
has walked from heaven to hell
meeting no-one on the path.

She makes camp after dark
and is gone before day breaks;
is a deserted island in her head,
a stopover on the endless way.

My paper aunt, for no extra charge,
will babysit herself in the evenings.
She spends extended periods of time
downtown, which has moved uptown.

There are perfectly logical reasons
for this but she cannot think of one.
She wasn't built for a life like hers,
is intense and serious about her art.

Evidence shows she is losing sleep,
often suffers from bouts of crying;
dreams don't make a lot of noise
but they have plenty of things to say.

My paper aunt embraces places
where she does not belong, turns
information over to anyone who asks
and is a citizen of every country

although she will never live there,
at least not for very long. She thinks
in silence, muffled fog bound echoes
a kind of storm warning to us all.

A story I once heard said the sunset
is only coloured paint on her canvas,
storms the jagged words she sings,
these poems her summer dress.

My paper aunt has few compulsions,
will try anything once. She has
dug out the wolf, filled the vacuum,
has always been a proper princess.

She made her own coffin several times
and often watches the world collapse.
This mother of mysteries took the moon
for a walk through everything in ruins

then became man of the match.
It is the same old same old that spins
inside her dervish art. She is a butterfly
in shadow, caught up in the mind's loop.

My paper aunt is old school,
will not sit out in the sun.
Her experiences are secondhand,
she prefers the indirect route

to wherever she wants to go,
is unsure of where that is. It is
a long walk home from everywhere
and the breath of unknowing often

descends, ready to blow her away
and blame it on the reason why.
How many more years of walking blind?
How many miles between the lines?

My paper aunt bottles it up,
spills it out when gravity pulls
outwards and downwards,
as rain in the wild calls out.

She is broken but still working,
queen of all returning sound,
guardian of the gates of sleep,
a rogue wave in the floating world.

Always in debt, she waits for the needle
to drop, so she can bury the ghost.
There is an impossible momentum
to every mistake she makes.

My paper aunt writes letters to herself,
exhibits her own paintings on the walls.
Roll on the rusty days of heavy metal
when thunder fills the heart, she says.

Nobody knows what that means.
If these trees ever learn to talk
we would cut them down to burn;
if life was an endless holiday

how would we take a break?
I have started to think that
perhaps the path does not exist,
that the door is a question mark.

My paper aunt worships in the cathedral
of doubt, praises the stones she walks upon
before she returns, lit up, to starry point.
It takes love to love yourself, she says,

you have to take your hands off the wheel
and trust to the eternal chant, the song
of the moon and sun. This could all be yours
if you learn to walk barefoot in the snow.

Memories come running to meet her
in the mirror of negative space. She is
a child of the storm on forgotten roads,
a spectre who forgot to breathe.

Sudden Impact

The party is over, she is going upstairs
in her blue dress, having danced all night
in light streaming in as golden energy,
glowing to an extent impossible today.

The static poetry of the moment
means there is no dialogue between us,
or Mary and the angel. Words hover
but we cannot hear what is not said.

The moment has broken down, seeing
has come into its own. It challenges
our imagination and inclines us toward
scarcely believing in God. One question

worries Mary more than anything but
her only answer is through obedience;
in history all solutions are tentative,
there is no guide to what comes next.

She must fashion a theology from dreams
and the death of her son, become radiant
in physical and spiritual beauty, or explore
the white tunnel some say is the entrance

to heaven. A hundred and fifty yards behind
her house is a world where flesh melts
and in her imagination a tiny white bird
narrates the sudden impact of the divine.

It comes to us all. We must look at what
we see, make up our minds, pay attention
to surfaces and the different ways they
catch the light through religious smoke.

Remarks on Colour

Emotion depends on the materials used:
the drawn line is a record of a gesture,
colour keeps within itself its own magic.

Devotees of painting will no doubt protest
it is not light that has been divided,
that structure is part of the whole.

Colours have psychological and moral overtones,
are vessels of a transcendental essence,
a synchronicity between the sonic and visual.

Silent moments recorded
then played back in a different order
might produce the sensation of white.

We don't have a visual memory for colour.
Form has a power of inner suggestion:
the silence of black is the silence of death.

Strange Photos

It Is

It is time for some straight talk.
It is all about the tilt of the Earth's axis.
It is not hard to cut it into two equal halves
which are linked like links of a chain.
It is easy to smudge the result.
It is impossible to know for sure,
it makes everything run.

It is trying to look at strange photos
and guess what they are.
It is an image vocabulary
that has been developed
to help children communicate
about a range of important issues.
It is the drowsy sleepy feeling
you get after eating a large meal.

It is obvious. It is unavailable.
It is bad news. It is electricity.
It is a possessive pronoun meaning
it is too late. It never is. It is
surprisingly simple. It is raining.
Life is unpredictable more than it seems;
it is the best thing anyone has ever done.

It is how we plan to do it. It is published
once a year and is available on request.
It is journalistically irresponsible:
it is very important that we give credit
where credit is due. It is possible
to group them into major categories.
It is safe to do so. It is an approach
that appears superficially attractive.

It is old before its time, it is falling
far below expectations. It is what it is:
it is the best controller we've ever made,
it is already running. It is impossible
to know for sure the extent of the connection,
it is no wonder that some creative people
step forward with truly innovative ideas.

You asked for it and here it is.

What It Is

What it is to be entirely alone in a field
and feel the sky suddenly come down.
What it is is surprisingly simple:
an all but lost phrase from another era,
a survey of self-reported reading times,
a research platform that gives you access
to objective content and powerful tools.
It is a stone with writing on it in two languages,
fragments of collage worked in to each page.

What it is is a continuation and culmination
of a long inquiry into many ideas;
it is trying to look at strange photos
and guess what they are.
Sleep deprivation affects the brain
in multiple ways, impairing judgment,
causing slow reaction times whilst
increasing the likelihood of drifting off
and enhancing the mood in your home.

It's a great way to stay on top
of what's happening now,
is used every day for a wide variety

of purposes by normal people.
But it is harder to read the signals
when you are old and on the way out.
It is like asking how and why
to use whom in a sentence,
or stopping the sky falling on your head.

Is It?

Is it too late? How late is too late?
Is it just me? How dare you embarrass
the author. *Is it art?* Let's not be too hard
on ourselves. *Is it real?* This type of memory
doesn't exist. *Is it because?* How can you tell?

Is it fair? No-one can tell the difference.
Is it dark outside? Extreme weather
is already happening. *Is it time to sleep?*
Body and language merge. *Is it in English?*
It is a unique digit combination.

Is it a medicinal product? Read the instructions.
Is it waste? It's a real biological condition.
Is it fun? Just give it time. *Is it dangerous?*
It's hard to know for sure. *Is it the internet age?*
Search everywhere and find out.

Is it right to waste helium on party balloons?
Letting you down was easy. *Is it ethical
to block adverts online?* I have done it
by breaking my computer. *Is it recycled?*
Pure, consistent, and reliably available.

Is it funny? It's funny because it's true.
Is it now? People remember the moment.

Is it necessary? No reboot is required. *Is it
different?* It is all we have come to expect.
Is it hazardous? There are often aftershocks.

Is it in the public domain? They are buried
in the ground. *Is it a cold or the flu?*
That goes without saying. *Is it possible?*
Think about what you're doing. *Is it edible?*
Enjoy a meal in the comfort of our lounge bar.

Is it worth being wise? Try to live at peace
with everyone. *Is it legal?* It's not a good idea
at all. *Is it a book?* A category will not change
the content. *Is it love or a list?* Practise making
and using the passive. *Is it contagious?*

Ours have been itchy. *Is it yours to give?*
Property is theft, so take it. *Is it time?*
For most people, no. *Is it normal?*
More or less. *Is it time to say goodbye?*
It is time to say goodbye.

What Is it Like?

'I don't know, but I do like the idea
of a chaotic moment inside a frame'
  —Charles Hayward

What is it like to be a bird?
Much more than can be analysed
or presented effectively. This poem
does not deal with the bird's brain;
most scientists are pretty regular people
who share everyday mediocrity.

What is it like in heaven?
When you first step off the plane
it is the heat you notice first.
The language spoken is not my native tongue,
but people are talking about
whether Aldi or Waitrose is a better option.
When people ask me 'Does everyone
seem dumb to you?' I say 'No' but think

What is it like to be a thermostat?
It can be construed as a model
of the world although it may not
seem like that at the time.
There is much we cannot know,
which is why current discussions
get it so obviously wrong.

*What is this place? What's different
about it? Is it different anymore?*
Good questions, every one.
The universe is so large
that stars bigger than our sun
look like tiny pinpoints of light
because they are so far away.
It is possible that some things
will lose their usefulness over time
but velcro is crucial to civilization,
is a force to be reckoned with.

Everyone handles it differently,
just like no-one grieves the same.
Simple tools help us all understand
what it's like to be someone else.
What's your typical day like?
That should be clear to anyone
who has heard a trumpet and seen red.

What is it like to see
something for the first time?
Look at these strange photos
and guess what they are.
Comparison is somewhat simplistic
but it illuminates different assumptions
and interpretations. *What exactly is*
third-hand smoke? Is it a crime
to plan or incite genocide, even before
killing starts? What is a strange loop
and what is it like to be one?

It's a waking nightmare where
you have all these bizarre images
of terrible things always happening.
It leaves you exhausted and unable
to think or find the right word.
Some of us have never known
a situation as frightening as this.

What is it like? Quite an experience;
a slow dance without an answer
and so many dumb ways to die.

Evidence

for David Hart

A folding set of postcards
and her handwritten journal
are how she remembers
the weeks we spent away.
There, the sun is different and
we have time to read books, to sit
and look at the distant sky and hills.
Here, I commandeer the patio table,
despite the morning mist,
and wonder what David meant
in his surprise email this morning
about whether or not it is possible
to write about faith today.

Renaissance angels may astound us
but they are not how we see
the world. We have different stories
and other ways to paint the words
we use to get to the bottom of things.
Our explanations are to do with science
and how things were first made, what
they will become. There is no room
for wonder or any sense of doubt;
the grey that fills the valley
is just moisture, not an obscuring veil,
and if we get a rainbow it is water
acting as a prism, not a sign from God.

Is she sure she was over there?
Yes, she has photos, and grandma
showed her others: so now I have a past
for her to visit and she knows a little more
about the grandfather she never met.
More recent evidence is only virtual data:

we never get to see printed pictures,
there is no photo album to leaf through.
Over there, there are angels on the walls
forever telling Mary she is blessed,
the sun always shines, the pool
is always blue, and the mist never lasts,
always burns away later in the day.

Notes

'"A Process of Discovery"'
>The title is a quote from David Miller.
>The Greek author was Yannis Ritsos.
>The four books were David Batchelor's *The Luminous and the Grey*, Jim Dodge's *Stone Junction*, Karl O. Knausgaard's *A Time to Every Purpose Under Heaven* and David Miller's *Reassembling Still – Collected Poems*.

Many of the annunciation and colour poems draw on the following source material:
>*Fra Angelico*, Diane Cole Ahl
>*Colour*, ed. David Batchelor
>*Chromophobia*, David Batchelor
>*The Luminous and the Grey*, David Batchelor
>*Painting the Word*, John Drury
>*Heaven*, Peter Stanford
>*What Colour is the Sacred?* Michael Taussig
>*Remarks on Colour*, Ludwig Wittgenstein

'Shadow Triptych'
>This prose poem sequence was and is for Brian Louis Pearce.
>It makes use of the following source material:
>Francis Bacon paintings, Hayward Gallery, February 1998
>*Francis Bacon and the Loss of Self*, Ernst van Alphen
>*Francis Bacon: In conversation with Michel Archimbaud*
>*The Trouble with Being Born*, E.M. Cioran,
>*Creation out of Nothing*, Don Cupitt
>*Mysticism after Modernity*, Don Cupitt
>*More Brilliant than the Sun*, Kodwo Eshun
>*Setting Our Sights by the Morning Star*, Hendrik Hart
>*A Search for Solitude*, Thomas Merton
>*A Wild Sheep Chase*, Haruki Murakami
>*Victoria Hammersmith*, Brian Louis Pearce
>*Cities for a Small Planet*, Richard Rogers
>*Space is the Place*, John F. Szwed
>*Imagologies*, Mark C. Taylor and Esa Saarinen

The poem 'Dear Mary' is assembled from the song lyrics of Creedence Clearwater Revival, Dido, The Faces, Patty Griffin, Her Name is Calla, Janis Joplin, Mary Mary, Elvis Presley, Bruce Springsteen, Porter Wagoner and Hank Williams Jr, and other texts.

'Shake the Angel'

Fra Angelico's *Annunciation* in Cortona has the angel's speech written in lines of gold text between Mary and the Angel.

'Strange Photos'

The first sentence of 'What It Is' is from David Grubb's poem 'What Are The Dead For'.

Acknowledgements

Some of these poems were first published in the following magazines:
Acumen, Caduceus, Establishment, international times, Local Nomad, The Matthew's House Project, New Mystics, Noon, Osiris, Shearsman, Tar, Tears in the Fence, Temenos Academy Review, Under the Radar, The Wardrobe, The Wayfarer, X-Peri. Thanks to the editors.

'Annunciations' and 'Hidden' were first published in *A Star in the Heart* (Christ Church Community Centre, 2014). Thanks to the editor, David Grubb.

'Cimabue' previously appeared in *Boombox* (Shearsman Books, 2009). Thanks to the publisher, Tony Frazer.

'Shadow Triptych' was first published by Maquette Press. Thank you to the publisher, Andy Brown.

'Distance' was exhibited as part of the mail art exhibition, *Hommage aan de wereld van Hokusai* in Merksplas, Belgium.

'Annunciation by Francis Bacon' was exhibited as part of the mail art exhibition, *A Dream of Francis Bacon*, in São Paulo, Brazil

'My Paper Aunt' was first published by Storm Warning as an illustrated booklet, with illustrations by Russell Kirk. Thank you Russell.

'Strange Photos' previously appeared in *Why we write/right outside the line?* (Lit Fest Press, 2016).

Thanks to Martin Caseley, Paul Sutton, Andy Brown, Harvey Hix, and especially David Hart and the late Margaret Pearce for advice and comments, and to Adrian and Debbie for use of their art.

And thanks to Jim for his perceptive and knowledgeable preface.

CPSIA information can be obtained
at www.ICGtesting.com
Printed in the USA
BVOW04s2234240417

482142BV00001B/40/P